SandCastle™

First Rhymes

Gwen the Hen

Kelly Doudna

Consulting Editor, Diane Craig, M.A./Reading Specialist

ABDO
Publishing Company

Published by ABDO Publishing Company, 4940 Viking Drive, Edina, Minnesota 55435.

Printed in the United States.

Credits
Edited by: Pam Price
Curriculum Coordinator: Nancy Tuminelly
Cover and Interior Design and Production: Mighty Media
Photo Credits: AbleStock, Corel, Photodisc, Stockbyte

Library of Congress Cataloging-in-Publication Data

Doudna, Kelly, 1963-
    Gwen the hen / Kelly Doudna.
        p. cm. -- (First rhymes)
    Includes index.
    ISBN 1-59679-487-9 (hardcover)
    ISBN 1-59679-488-7 (paperback)
        1. English language--Rhyme--Juvenile literature. I. Title. II. Series.
PE1517.D683 2005
808.1--dc22
                                                                        2005048791

SandCastle™ books are created by a professional team of educators, reading specialists, and content developers around five essential components that include phonemic awareness, phonics, vocabulary, text comprehension, and fluency. All books are written, reviewed, and leveled for guided reading and early intervention reading, and designed for use in shared, guided, and independent reading and writing activities to support a balanced approach to literacy instruction.

Let Us Know

After reading the book, SandCastle would like you to tell us your stories about reading. What is your favorite page? Was there something hard that you needed help with? Share the ups and downs of learning to read. We want to hear from you! To get posted on the ABDO Publishing Company Web site, send us e-mail at:

sandcastle@abdopub.com

SandCastle Level: Beginning

den

hen

pen

10

ten

wren

I see a .

I like the .

See the  .

This is a **10**.

We see a  .

A fox is in the den.

The hen is white.

A pig is in the pen.

10

The ten is blue.

The wren is brown.

Gwen the Hen

Gwen is a hen.

16

Gwen the hen
lives in a pen.

18

Gwen the hen
leaves her pen
each morning at ten.

Each morning at ten
when Gwen the hen
leaves her pen,
she passes the den
of a fox named Len.

Gwen the hen
leaves her pen at ten
and passes Len's den
on her way to see Ben,
who is a wren.

About SandCastle™

A professional team of educators, reading specialists, and content developers created the SandCastle™ series to support young readers as they develop reading skills and strategies and increase their general knowledge. The SandCastle™ series has four levels that correspond to early literacy development in young children. The levels are provided to help teachers and parents select the appropriate books for young readers.

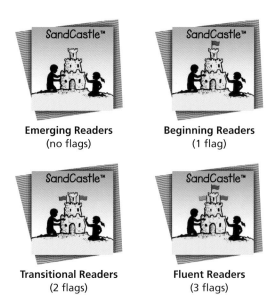

Emerging Readers
(no flags)

Beginning Readers
(1 flag)

Transitional Readers
(2 flags)

Fluent Readers
(3 flags)

These levels are meant only as a guide. All levels are subject to change.

To see a complete list of SandCastle™ books and other nonfiction titles from ABDO Publishing Company, visit **www.abdopub.com** or contact us at:

4940 Viking Drive, Edina, Minnesota 55435 • 1-800-800-1312 • fax: 1-952-831-1632